This book belongs to:

Joey Welch

Our Planet

© 2010 Top That! Publishing plc
This 2011 edition published by Sandy Creek, by arrangement with Top That! Publishing plc

Sandy Creek
122 Fifth Avenue, New York, NY 10011
ISBN-13: 978-1-4351-3199-6
Printed and bound in Guangdong, China
Manufactured April 2011
Lot 1 3 5 7 9 10 8 6 4 2

CONTENTS

CONTENTS

ORIGINS OF EARTH

Our planet is one of eight planets circling the Sun. Our whole solar system is just one of many millions in a vast universe.

How old is Earth

 Earth was formed around 4.7 billion years ago

 Dinosaurs arrived around 250 million years ago

 Humans (Homo Sapiens) arrived around 250,000 years ago

Imagine "time" as represented by the distance between your outstretched arms. The universe was formed on your longest left-hand finger. One-cell lifeforms began between your wrist and your elbow. Dinosaurs did not appear until you reach your right hand. Humans arrived on the fingernail of your longest right-hand finger!

Was there life on Earth from the beginning

Definitely not! At first, Earth's surface was far too hot to support any form of life. Gradually, however, it cooled down so that a thin crust formed round the outside. It remained boiling hot inside—and is still the same today!

When did life on Earth start

The oldest microfossil found so far is 3,500 million years old. Life began about 1,000 million years after Earth was formed. Scientists tend to date the age of rocks to give us clues to Earth's age, working on a "calendar" that spans millions of years.

How was Earth formed

One theory is that Earth formed from a gigantic cloud of spinning gas and dust. Here's what is thought to have happened.

A floating cloud of gas and dust was sent spinning by an exploding star.

Gases formed inside the spinning cloud to form a new star—our Sun.

The remaining dust continued to spin around the Sun, forming the planets.

The planets collided and were sent spinning into their orbits.

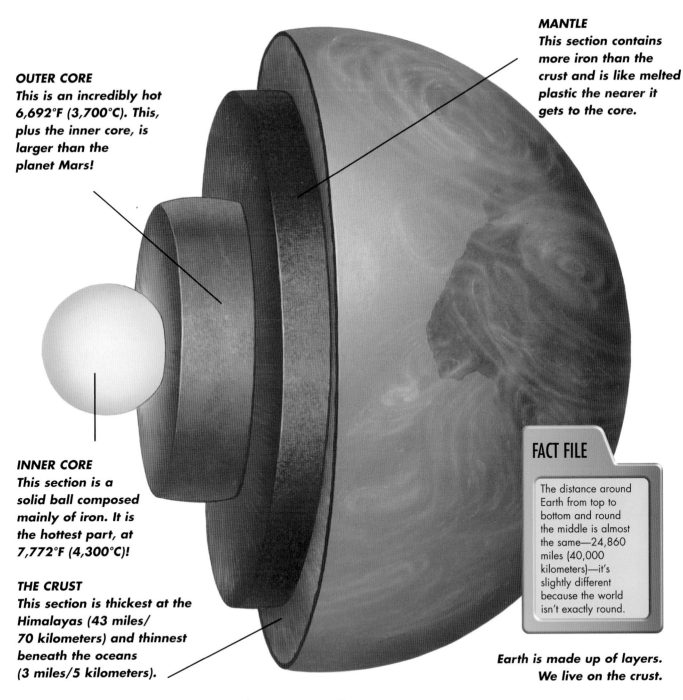

OUTER CORE
This is an incredibly hot 6,692°F (3,700°C). This, plus the inner core, is larger than the planet Mars!

MANTLE
This section contains more iron than the crust and is like melted plastic the nearer it gets to the core.

INNER CORE
This section is a solid ball composed mainly of iron. It is the hottest part, at 7,772°F (4,300°C)!

THE CRUST
This section is thickest at the Himalayas (43 miles/ 70 kilometers) and thinnest beneath the oceans (3 miles/5 kilometers).

FACT FILE

The distance around Earth from top to bottom and round the middle is almost the same—24,860 miles (40,000 kilometers)—it's slightly different because the world isn't exactly round.

Earth is made up of layers. We live on the crust.

5

THE SUN

Our Sun was formed billions of years ago. All the planets in the solar system orbit around the sun, and it provides warmth and light to Earth. Despite being very old, both the surface of the Sun and its interior are hotbeds of activity.

How big is the Sun

The Sun is truly massive. To give you some idea, it is 110 times wider than Earth and you could fit Earth into the Sun about 1,300,000 times! Interestingly, the temperature of the Sun's surface is about the same as at Earth's core.

How hot is the Sun

As you would expect from such a gigantic fireball, the temperature is blazing hot. The center of the Sun is estimated to be around 59 million degrees fahrenheit (15 million degrees centigrade). That's hot enough to melt absolutely anything instantly!

What is the Sun made of and how does it work

The Sun started as a rotating cloud of gas and dust. This rotation flattened the cloud and pressed the dust together in the center so that it became a larger lump. Once enough matter had been pressed together, the lump became larger, very dense (squashed) and very hot! Once the heat reached a certain point, nuclear reactions began and the star, our Sun, was born! The nuclear reactions at the Sun's center create enough pressure to prevent the Sun collapsing.

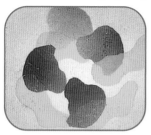

The Sun started as a cloud of dust and gas and formed a large ball.

After the Sun was formed, dust around it clumped together, forming planets.

Earth relies on the Sun's heat and light to sustain life on its surface.

FACT FILE

From the earliest times, humans have realized the need for the Sun to sustain life. The Aztecs of ancient Mexico, the Incas of Peru and the ancient Egyptians all worshipped the Sun as a god.

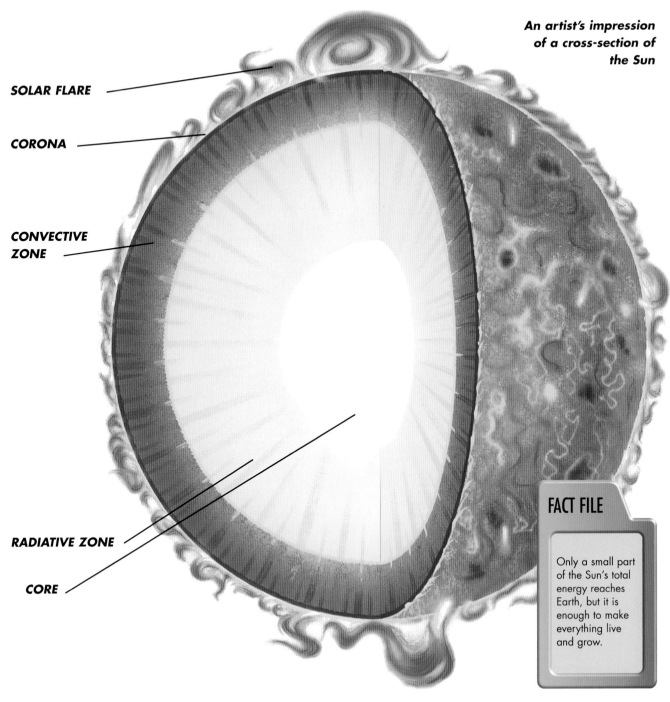

SOLAR FLARE

CORONA

CONVECTIVE ZONE

RADIATIVE ZONE

CORE

An artist's impression of a cross-section of the Sun

FACT FILE

Only a small part of the Sun's total energy reaches Earth, but it is enough to make everything live and grow.

7

What is the difference between a sun and a star

Nothing! A sun is a burning star that gives out light. So, by looking at the night sky, you can see that the Sun is not alone in being a star. All those twinkling pinpoints of light are other stars in other galaxies, giving out heat and light just as our Sun does!

How long will our Sun last

The Sun will burn out eventually, but don't worry—it's not going to happen just yet. Scientists estimate that the Sun will have used up all its energy in about 7,000 million years time!

WARNING

Don't try looking for sunspots or solar flares. You should never look at the Sun through a telescope or with the naked eye. It can damage your eyesight and even make you go blind.

What are all those black spots

Sunspots are dark patches on the surface of the Sun. They appear black because these areas are not as hot as the gas surrounding them. Some sunspots are around 150 times larger than Earth! Bright clouds of helium, called faculae, occur above the areas where sunspots are about to form. Solar flares are bright loops of hot gas emerging from the areas of the Sun where sunspots are present. A flare can last from a few seconds to several hours.

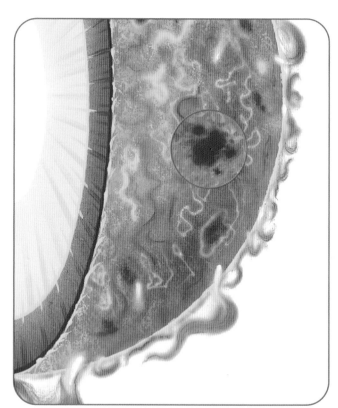

A sunspot on the surface of the Sun

THE ATMOSPHERE

You can't see Earth's atmosphere, but it is the layer between Earth and outer space. It is delicate and under threat from the use of chemicals here on Earth. At present, scientists do not know of any other planet which has an atmosphere like ours.

What exactly is Earth's atmosphere

The special layer surrounding Earth is up to 621 miles (1,000 kilometers) thick and is held in place by Earth's gravity. It is made from many gases, including oxygen and carbon dioxide. Life on Earth depends on this combination of gases.

What are the northern lights (aurora borealis)

Particles heading to Earth from the Sun join together in a ribbon called a solar wind. Some particles become charged and are forced down into Earth's atmosphere where they collide and react with gases. This causes the ions to glow red, violet, green and blue. These displays are most often seen at the Poles (hence the northern/southern lights), where they can occur around 200 times per year!

- 21% oxygen
- 0.9% argon
- 0.03% carbon dioxide
- 0.07% other gases
- 78% nitrogen

FACT FILE

When a space shuttle returns to Earth from orbit, it has to pass through the atmosphere. The heavier air causes the spacecraft to become very hot and heat shields need to be used to prevent it burning up.

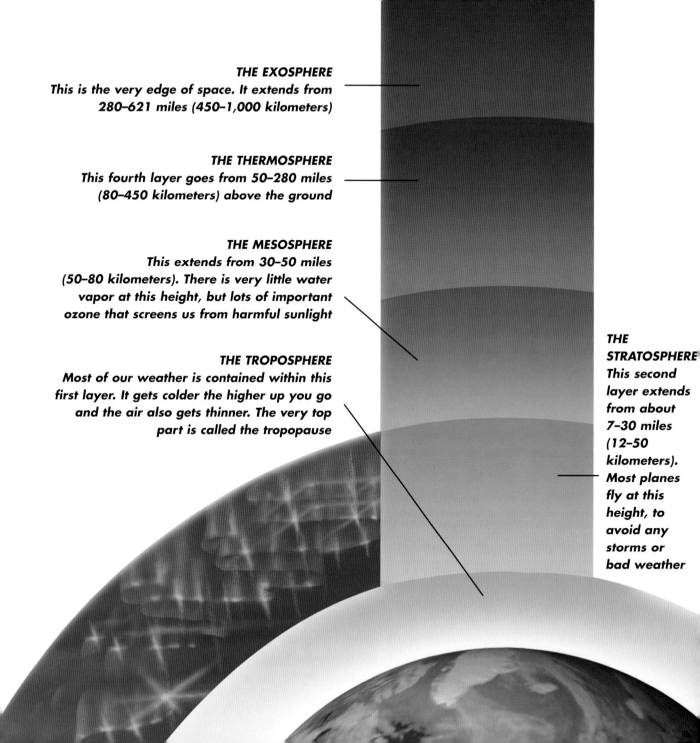

THE EXOSPHERE
This is the very edge of space. It extends from
280–621 miles (450–1,000 kilometers)

THE THERMOSPHERE
This fourth layer goes from 50–280 miles
(80–450 kilometers) above the ground

THE MESOSPHERE
This extends from 30–50 miles
(50–80 kilometers). There is very little water
vapor at this height, but lots of important
ozone that screens us from harmful sunlight

THE TROPOSPHERE
Most of our weather is contained within this
first layer. It gets colder the higher up you go
and the air also gets thinner. The very top
part is called the tropopause

**THE
STRATOSPHERE**
This second
layer extends
from about
7–30 miles
(12–50
kilometers).
Most planes
fly at this
height, to
avoid any
storms or
bad weather

What is the atmosphere made of

Earth's atmosphere is made up of five different layers—the troposphere, the stratosphere, the mesophere, the thermosphere and the exosphere. If you were an astronaut blasting off in a spaceship, you would pass through these five layers described on the left.

Why is the sky blue

Light is made up of a whole spectrum of colors which blend together. Light also has different wavelengths, the longest of which is found at the red end of the spectrum, with the shortest at the blue end. When sunlight enters the atmosphere, it collides with oxygen and nitrogen atoms which "scatter" different wavelengths, the shorter, blue ones being the most affected. This results in our perception that the sky is blue.

Why does the sky change color

At sunrise and sunset, the Sun is very low in the sky. This makes light strike the atmosphere at a different angle, scattering different wavelengths of light. So, at these times of day, the sky appears as beautiful shades of red, yellow and orange.

FACT FILE

Neil Armstrong, the first man to walk on the Moon in July 1969, said Earth looked like "a splendid jewel suspended in space". Seen from space, the beautiful appearance of Earth is caused by sunlight reflecting off the oceans.

WATER

Did you know that the glass of water that you drank today could once have been used to wash Shakespeare's feet? Water is circulated in one of nature's most impressive systems, the water cycle, which is described here.

Where does it all start

We can start the cycle by imagining a rain cloud about to burst. The water rushes to Earth, making its first stop at the surface of mountains. Some of it is stored here where it freezes. The rest flows down into streams which become rivers. This river water flows into massive reservoirs where some is taken away by pipes to the water supply works to be used as drinking water. The rivers also take some water to the sea. However, some water collects elsewhere on the ground.

How much water is on Earth

Seventy percent of Earth's surface is covered by water, most of which is salty and found in the seas and oceans. Only two percent of the world's water is suitable to drink or to water crops. As most of this is frozen in the ice caps, it's no wonder that we recycle water whenever we can. Water cannot ever be created or destroyed—it just gets stored in different ways.

Why are oceans salty

If you filled a dishpan with water from the sea, it would contain around 1 lb (450 g) of salt. The same amount of water from a freshwater source would contain about 0.01 lb (5 g) of salt! Even though the seas and oceans are fed by freshwater rivers, they contain salt from other sources, such as broken up rocks, worn-down mountains and gases that have escaped from Earth's crust.

Oceans get salt from Earth's crust

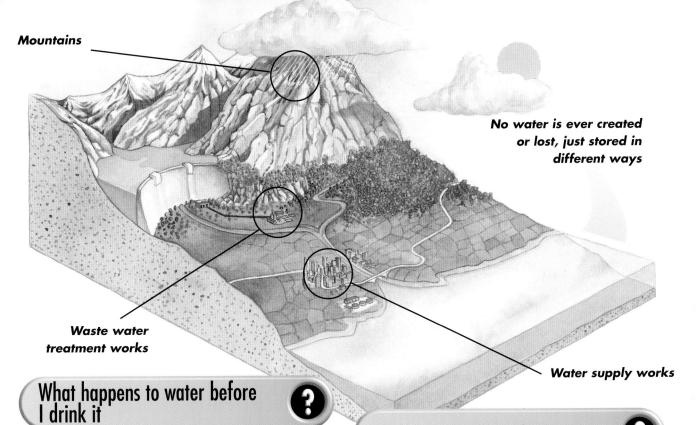

Mountains

**No water is ever created
or lost, just stored in
different ways**

**Waste water
treatment works**

Water supply works

What happens to water before I drink it ?

The water we drink is usually taken from rivers by pipes and stored either on the surface in reservoirs, or under the ground. At the water supply works, a substance is added to make any large pieces of dirt stick together, which are then lifted out. The water is filtered again, and chemicals are added before it is pumped along a network of pipes and up through our taps.

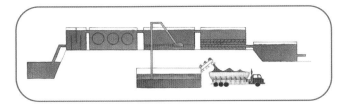

The water supply works treat our drinking water

What causes rain and snow ?

The water droplets inside a cloud move around and bang into each other, causing them to stick together and get bigger. When they become too heavy for the atmosphere to support their weight, they "fall out" of the cloud. If this happens when it is warm, the water droplets remain liquid and rain falls. When it's really cold and the droplets get colder on the way down to Earth they freeze to become snow. Water falls in all of its different forms, landing on Earth's surface. This is known as precipitation. We're now back to the beginning of the cycle!

MOUNTAINS

Around 300 million years ago, two supercontinents called Laurasia and Gondwanaland, which had been moving towards each other at a rate of several centimeters a year, crashed, buckling with great force, forming mountains...

What is a mountain range

"Range" is the name given to a group of mountains. The Alps make up a range of mountains, passing through six countries in total. The highest point is Mont Blanc (15,770 feet/4,807 meters) which is situated between France and Italy. The Rockies are a range of mountains situated in North America, stretching from Canada to central Mexico. Mount Everest, in the Himalayas mountains in South Asia, is the highest place on Earth. It is 29,070 feet (8,863 meters) above sea level.

The Rockies, Colorado

What are tectonic plates

The supercontinents that crashed together formed a single land mass called Pangea. This broke apart to form the continents. These gigantic pieces of Earth's jigsaw are called tectonic plates, which float on top of a layer of magma. Geologists know that the plates still move at several centimeters per year!

How are mountains formed

If you could look inside a mountain, you would see that the rock inside look crumpled. Fossils found on the tips of mountains are often those of sea animals. These two things make scientists believe that mountains were formed by very powerful forces pushing huge rocks from the seabed upwards to form the mountains. These forces are still moving under our feet, but so slowly that you will never notice!

What is an underwater mountain

In some oceans, the tops of underwater mountains poke out above the surface making steep islands. One mountain in the Pacific Ocean, Mauna Loa, is actually much bigger than Mount Everest when measured from the sea bed.

Mauna Loa is a volcano in the Pacific Ocean

FACT FILE

Geologists believe that the plates of India and Asia were once separated by sea, and that the Himalayas mountain range formed when they drifted together and struck one another. This took place around 600,000 years ago—which makes the Himalayas fairly young!

RIVERS

All rivers start from high ground, whether they are slow-flowing or torrential. The journey downhill is often a long one, and the river will change direction and size on the way.

What is a river's source

The source of a river is where it begins. The source of the Ganges, a major river in the Indian subcontinent, is at the Gangotri Glacier, a massive block of ice situated in the Himalayas.

What is a river's estuary

Huge ports are built around estuaries, where the river flows out to meet the sea. They contain brackish water, a mix of fresh and salt water, and are affected by the sea's tides.

Which is the longest river

The Nile in Africa is the longest—but not by much. It measures 4,157 miles (6,690 kilometers) from one end to the other. Close behind comes the Amazon in South America which stretches for 4,000 miles (6,437 kilometers). The Yangtze in China comes third, followed by the Mississippi in North America. These are the world's "big four" rivers.

What can we use rivers for

Rivers can be very useful for transporting goods. The Ohio River connects Lake Erie with a vast network of inland rivers that bring coal and petroleum products to, and from, America's major cities. Huge loads can be carried on barges which are able to take goods a long way inland. In certain parts of the world where it is too wet to build roads, rivers are used exactly as roads are, with boats being the replacements for cars. Venice is known as the "City of Canals" because of its water-based transport system. River water is used to provide life. Bangladesh sits on approximately 700 rivers, and although floods have negative effects, the silt deposits fertilize the soil and the fish can be eaten as a source of protein.

Venice's canals provide a water-based transport system

Ships bring goods inland

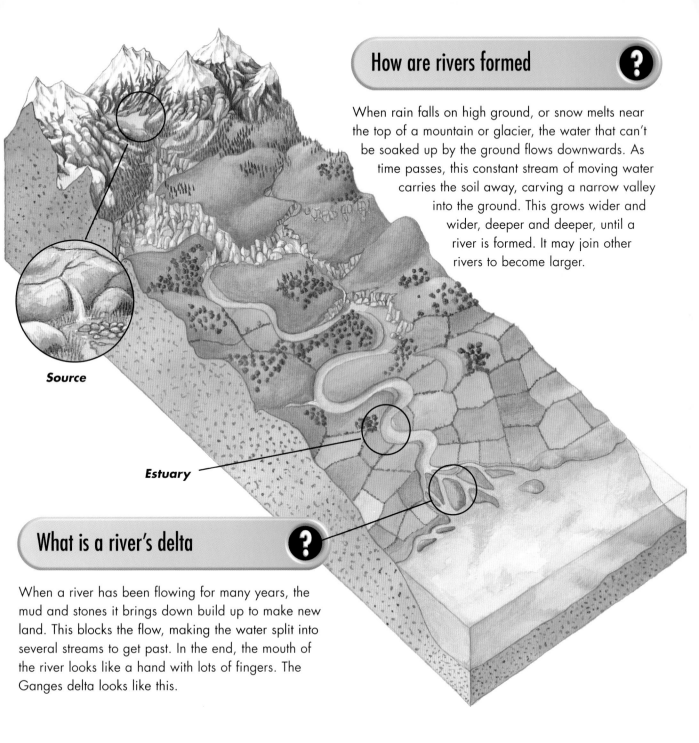

How are rivers formed ?

When rain falls on high ground, or snow melts near the top of a mountain or glacier, the water that can't be soaked up by the ground flows downwards. As time passes, this constant stream of moving water carries the soil away, carving a narrow valley into the ground. This grows wider and wider, deeper and deeper, until a river is formed. It may join other rivers to become larger.

Source

Estuary

What is a river's delta ?

When a river has been flowing for many years, the mud and stones it brings down build up to make new land. This blocks the flow, making the water split into several streams to get past. In the end, the mouth of the river looks like a hand with lots of fingers. The Ganges delta looks like this.

ELECTRIC SKIES

With a bolt averaging a length of 3 miles (5 kilometers) and a temperature four times hotter than the Sun, it is no wonder that lightning is one of the most dramatic of all nature's phenomena.

What causes a thunderstorm

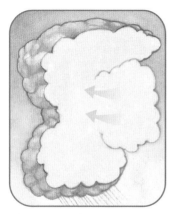

In a word—electricity! Cumulonimbus clouds (see page 30) build up in the sky. These rain-bearing clouds usually produce showers, but they can gather together to produce more serious downpours.

These clouds grow vertically instead of horizontally

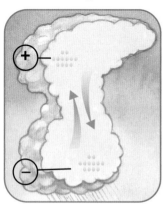

Inside these vast clouds, water droplets form static electricity by swirling around and bumping into each other. The positively charged water droplets gather at the top of the cloud, while the negatively charged ones sink to the bottom.

Negatively charged water droplets sink to the bottom of the cloud

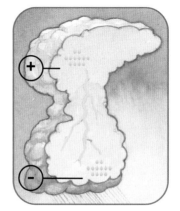

Eventually, the difference between the positively and negatively charged droplets becomes so great that electricity flashes from one to the other. This is called sheet lightning and it passes through the cloud.

Electricity (lightning) flashes between the charged droplets

The ground below is also negatively charged, so electricity flashes down from the cloud to the ground. This makes the much more dangerous fork lightning. Finally, these massive discharges of electricity heat up the air inside the storm clouds. The air expands so quickly that it explodes, causing the tremendous rumbling and crashing noise that we call thunder.

Tall objects, like trees, are prime targets for a lightning strike

Is it safe to get into a car during a storm

A car is one of the safer places to be if you can't get indoors. However, this is not due to the rubber tires which are commonly believed to insulate you from the ground. (When something is an "insulator" it means that forces of electricity or heat cannot pass through it very easily.) The reason the car protects you is due to its metal shell. Metal is a conductor, meaning the electricity runs straight through it, taking lightning to the ground. Just make sure you don't touch the metal!

Shelter in a car—but don't touch the metal sides!

Who was Benjamin Franklin

In 1752, politician and scientist Benjamin Franklin proved that lightning was made of electricity by flying a kite in a thunderstorm. It had a metal key attached to it and the electricity was seen sparking off the end. (This was a highly dangerous experiment and people who tried to repeat it were killed by lightning strikes!)

How far away is the storm

When you see a flash of lightning, count the number of seconds before you hear the following rumble of thunder. If there's a long gap, the storm is a long way away. If it's short, the storm is almost overhead. (If you want to be more accurate, every two seconds is the equivalent of half a mile away / one kilometer.)

FACT FILE

Light travels much faster than sound. Therefore, we see the flash of lightning before we hear the clap of thunder that it has caused.

EARTHQUAKES

Earth's crust is not a smooth coating like an eggshell but a restless, shifting surface from which huge tremors can come with little warning.

What causes an earthquake

Earth's crust has lots of huge cracks in it which make the land in between look like tiles. These massive sections, called plates, move and rub together, building up pressure. Most of the pressure is absorbed by rocks, but when it gets too much, trouble starts. The plates shatter at their weakest point, releasing enormous amounts of energy which radiate outwards as shock waves, making a large area of ground shake violently. These are called seismic waves. Most damage occurs near the middle of the earthquake which is called the epicenter.

Can we predict earthquakes

Not exactly, but scientists who study earthquakes can isolate several warning signs. The normal pattern of seismic waves starts to speed up, and swelling can be detected in the ground. Lots of tiny tremors occur along the junction of Earth's plates. As with volcanoes, it is important to look at the history surrounding the area where earthquakes have happened in the past to try to establish patterns in the size of the "shocks". This is one of the reasons that seismologists record even the tiniest tremors that would go unnoticed by us.

What happens afterwards

Tremors often continue after the main quake, making rescue work even more difficult. These lesser, follow-up tremors are called aftershocks. On 12th January 2010, an earthquake measuring 7.0 on the Richter Scale shook Haiti in the Caribbean. By the 24th January, at least 52 aftershocks had been recorded.

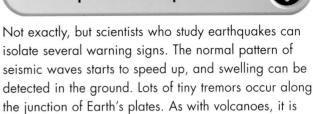

FACT FILE

When earthquakes occur under the sea, they cause gigantic waves, called tsunamis, and can cause huge incoming waves (wrongly called "tidal waves"). Although rare, they can cause massive damage. An earthquake in March 1964 caused a Pacific-wide tsunami, with waves reaching a height of 104 feet (31.7 meters) above low tide in Whittier, Alaska.

Continental crust—forms the thinnest, topmost layer of Earth's surface and is mainly rock.

An earthquake occurs when tectonic plates move and rub against one another, building pressure deep within Earth.

Lithosphere—around 155 miles (250 km) thick, this layer is rigid at the top and softer when it descends into the upper mantle.

Asthenosphere—mainly formed from the upper mantle and is a layer of thick fluid.

When scientists study earthquakes, they need to look at Earth's layers in more detail

How do we measure earthquakes

In 1935, Charles Richter devised a simple scale to indicate the size of an earthquake from 0–10. Anything under 3.5 would not be felt but is recorded. Under 6 would cause slight damage to a well-made building. Over 7 means a great earthquake.

What was the biggest earthquake

The largest recorded earthquake in the world took place in Chile in 1960, measuring 9.5 on the Richter Scale. One of the most deadly earthquakes took place in the Mediterranean in 1201 killing over one million people. Most of the world's earthquakes occur in a zone known as the Pacific Plate. This is due to the tectonic plate beneath the Pacific Ocean.

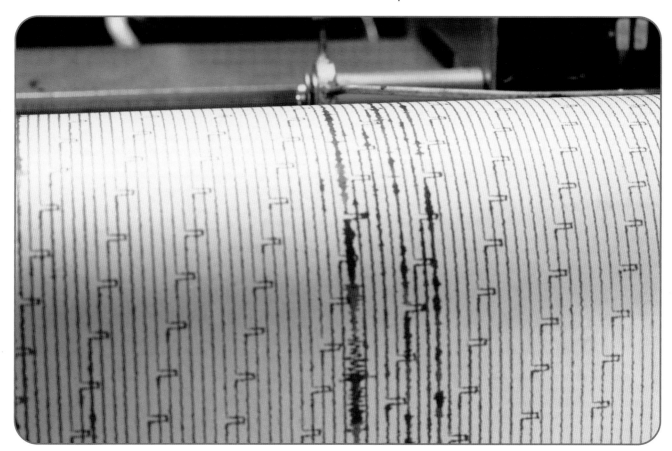

A seismometer is used to measure earthquakes

VOLCANOES

Volcanoes are a constant reminder of the awesome power of the molten magma that sits just 25 miles (40 kilometers) below Earth's surface.

What makes a volcano erupt

Just 25 miles (40 kilometers) beneath our feet, Earth is a bubbling mass of liquid rock so hot it will melt anything it touches. This molten rock is called magma. Most of the time Earth's crust keeps this magma well underground, but sometimes magma finds one of those faults in the crust. Then it has a chance to escape! Magma from inside Earth is subject to enormous pressure. It is also full of explosive gases. So when it finds a weak spot (usually between two plates), it surges upwards and gushes out into the air with terrific power.

What are the world's most famous volcanoes

Mount Vesuvius, Southern Italy
This volcano has an elevation of 4,200 feet (1,281 meters) and famously erupted in 79AD, wiping out the ancient Roman city of Pompeii.

Mount Etna, Sicily
This dormant volcano is huge and dominates the island of Sicily in the Mediterranean.

Krakatoa, East Java in Indonesia
This volcano erupted in 1883, causing the loudest explosion ever heard in the world. It also set off a tsunami that drowned 36,000 people and caused unusually high tides as far away as Britain!

For how long do volcanoes continue to erupt

When a volcano often erupts, it is called active. The world's most active volcano is Kilauea on the island of Hawaii. Eruptions started in January 1983 and show no sign of slowing down. If a volcano hasn't erupted for a long time by human standards (perhaps several hundred years) but still could do so, it is said to be dormant. The Mexican volcano, Paricutin, erupted between 1943 and 1952 and has been dormant ever since. If a volcano has finished erupting and won't do so again, it is extinct. The city of Edinburgh in Scotland is located on an extinct volcano. The geographical conditions have changed so greatly since the event (during the Carboniferous Period, about 250,000,000 years ago) that there's no danger that it will erupt again!

What is lava

Underneath Earth's crust is a layer of hot liquid rock called magma. When it spews from the top or the sides of a volcano, we call it lava. At first, it has the texture of melted plastic, but it gradually cools and turns to solid rock.

Lava... liquid to solid

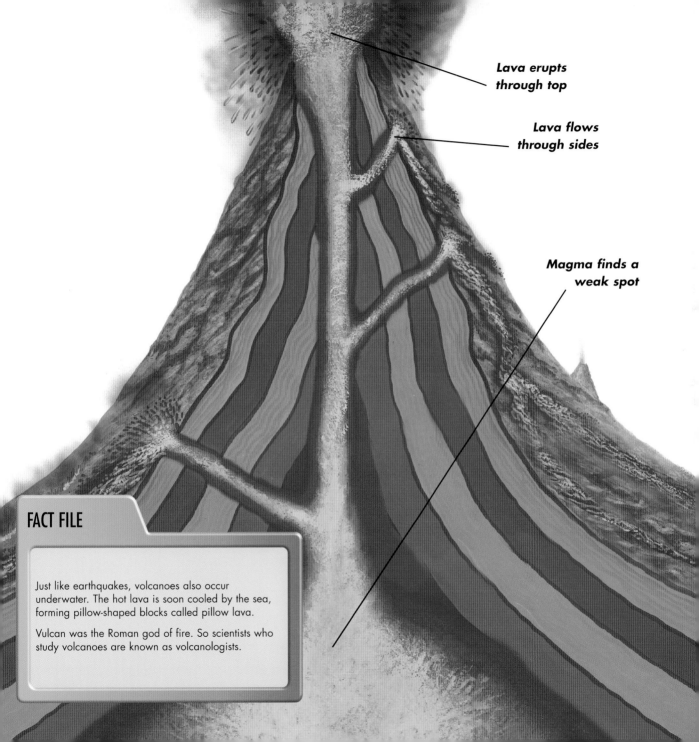

Lava erupts through top

Lava flows through sides

Magma finds a weak spot

FACT FILE

Just like earthquakes, volcanoes also occur underwater. The hot lava is soon cooled by the sea, forming pillow-shaped blocks called pillow lava.

Vulcan was the Roman god of fire. So scientists who study volcanoes are known as volcanologists.

WIND

As long as Earth keeps turning, there will be wind. Some places in the world experience tornadoes and hurricanes more frequently than others. Wind can cause chaos and destruction, but can also be harnessed to provide energy.

Why does the wind blow

The movement of air (wind) is caused by two things—differences in temperature on Earth and the fact that Earth is always rotating. The Sun does not heat Earth evenly. Its rays are much more intense at the equator and the surface here is much hotter than at the North and South Poles.

What is the eye of a hurricane

In the very center of a swirling hurricane, there is an area where it is quite calm. The eye of a hurricane can range from 2 miles (3 km) to 230 miles (370 km) across.

The eye of the hurricane

What exactly is a hurricane

Hurricanes are storm-force winds that build up over the sea. The moist air rises upwards and cold air rushes in. The strong wind caused by this starts to spin because of Earth's rotation. When this spinning wind builds up, it becomes a swirling monster up to 1,243 miles (2,000 kilometers) across, often reaching speeds of over 74 mph (120 kph).

Hurricanes can cause mass destruction

The Sun warms Earth, getting hottest around the equator. Warm air rises to the Poles. (1)

Air blowing from the North Pole causes the wind to blow from north to south (northerly wind). (3)

Westerly and easterly winds blow because Earth never stops spinning. The middle of Earth (the equator) spins faster than the top and bottom (the poles).

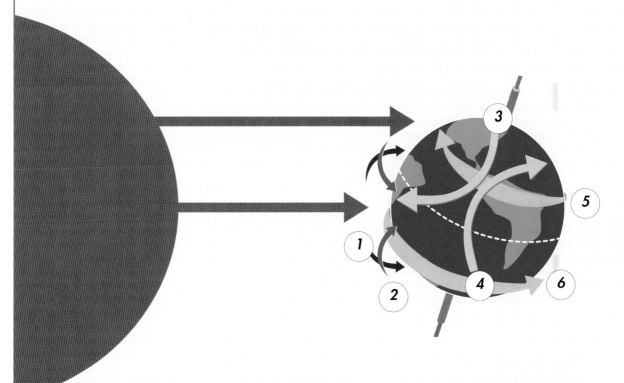

Cold air from the poles rushes in to fill the empty space. (2)

Air blowing from the South Pole causes the wind to blow from south to north (southerly wind). (4)

Air traveling towards the equator is pulled westwards (5) and air that is traveling towards the poles is pulled eastwards. (6)

Wind is caused by temperature and rotation

What is a tornado

Tornadoes form over land (not water). Rain clouds meet and start to spin as a result of Earth's rotation. These swirling clouds, or "twisters", form into giant funnel shapes that move along at terrifying speeds—up to 300 mph (480 kph).

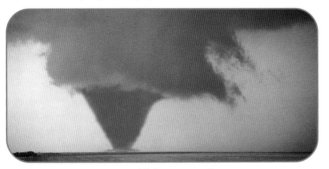

Twisters move at terrifying speeds

What is the Beaufort scale

This is a scale, invented by a British admiral called Sir Francis Beaufort in 1805, which divides the speed of the wind into twelve graded strengths.

Beaufort number	Wind speed (mph)	Seaman's term	Beaufort number	Wind speed (mph)	Seaman's term
0	Under 1	Calm	6	25–31	Strong breeze
1	1–3	Light air	7	32–38	Moderate gale
2	4–7	Light breeze	8	39–46	Fresh gale
3	8–12	Gentle breeze	9	47–54	Strong gale
4	13–18	Moderate breeze	10	55–63	Whole gale
5	19–24	Fresh breeze	11	64–72	Violent Storm
			12	73 or higher	Hurricane force

 # RAIN

Rain, rain, go away... once you have read the information on these pages, you will know what kind of rain you can expect simply by looking at the shapes of clouds.

What is rain, and how does it get there ?

Rain is water that has been drawn up into the sky by the Sun's heat and returns to the ground when it cools. This process is called the water cycle. For more on the water cycle, see pages 16–17.

How are rain clouds formed ?

A rain cloud forms in distinct stages. At stage three, the process happens very quickly and rain can start to fall in a matter of hours!

1. The Sun shines on open water, drawing vapor into the air.

2. As this water vapor rises upwards, it cools down and condenses.

3. Droplets gather together to form clouds, which join together with one another, making bigger and heavier cloud banks in the sky.

4. When the rain clouds become full of heavy droplets, they fall back to Earth in the form of rain (or hail and snow if the air is very cold.)

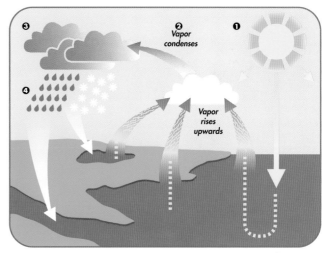

The water cycle

FACT FILE

Rainbows occur when rain falls at the same time as the Sun shines. Each raindrop splits the sunlight into its spectrum of colors like a prism. This happens right across the sky, picking up the shape of Earth and giving the rainbow its distinctive curved appearance. Legend has it that there is a pot of gold at the end of the rainbow—but nobody will ever find it because rainbows have no end!

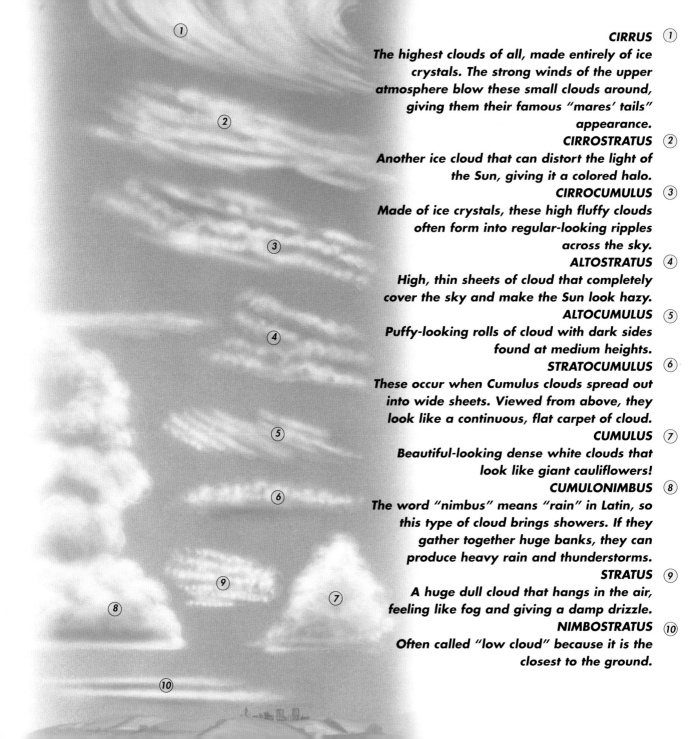

CIRRUS ①

The highest clouds of all, made entirely of ice crystals. The strong winds of the upper atmosphere blow these small clouds around, giving them their famous "mares' tails" appearance.

CIRROSTRATUS ②

Another ice cloud that can distort the light of the Sun, giving it a colored halo.

CIRROCUMULUS ③

Made of ice crystals, these high fluffy clouds often form into regular-looking ripples across the sky.

ALTOSTRATUS ④

High, thin sheets of cloud that completely cover the sky and make the Sun look hazy.

ALTOCUMULUS ⑤

Puffy-looking rolls of cloud with dark sides found at medium heights.

STRATOCUMULUS ⑥

These occur when Cumulus clouds spread out into wide sheets. Viewed from above, they look like a continuous, flat carpet of cloud.

CUMULUS ⑦

Beautiful-looking dense white clouds that look like giant cauliflowers!

CUMULONIMBUS ⑧

The word "nimbus" means "rain" in Latin, so this type of cloud brings showers. If they gather together huge banks, they can produce heavy rain and thunderstorms.

STRATUS ⑨

A huge dull cloud that hangs in the air, feeling like fog and giving a damp drizzle.

NIMBOSTRATUS ⑩

Often called "low cloud" because it is the closest to the ground.

What kinds of clouds are there

Clouds are little drops of water or ice crystals suspended in the atmosphere. There are ten different cloud formations recognized by scientists. They were first classified by an amateur weather expert called Luke Howard who spent his life observing clouds and their different characteristics.

What causes a flood

Floods occur when there is more rain than the ground can absorb. They can also be a result of extra high tides and natural disasters like earthquakes, volcanic eruptions, hurricanes and tornadoes. Global warming also causes flooding, forcing sea levels to rise, swamping any low-lying coastline.

When water has nowhere else to go...

SNOW AND ICE

Snow, like rain, can be a mixed blessing. It provides water when it melts from high ground, homes for both humans and animals, and a fabulous winter playground for children. Yet too much of it can cause chaos, disaster and loss of life...

What makes it snow

When the temperature of the air below a cloud reaches freezing point or beneath, water droplets in the cloud form ice crystals. When other droplets falling from the cloud bump into the ice crystals, they stick together, forming larger crystals (snowflakes).

Ice crystals stick together to form snowflakes

FACT FILE

Normally, things contract when they are made colder and expand when they warm up. Water, however works the other way around—it gets larger as it gets cooler (which is why ice in your soda floats and doesn't sink). Scientists think that this is due to water particles having a different shape to other liquids—the molecules in a block of ice are organized in tightly joined patterns which means its volume expands but its density decreases.

What shape are snowflakes

Snowflakes are hexagonal. Large, fluffy flakes are formed when the air below a cloud is slightly warmer than 32°F (0°C), so the falling ice crystals melt slightly, then clump together. If the air around a cloud is constantly 32°F (0°C) or below, then the crystals do not melt and fall in a shower of much smaller flakes—known as powder snow.

As snowflakes melt, they form more "dendrites" (branches)

How are snow and ice different

Snow is made up of snowflakes which have a lot of air in between them. Ice is solid frozen water. You can turn snow into ice by scooping a handful and pressing it together, getting rid of the air.

How do people live in the cold

The Inuit (native peoples of the Arctic) have turned their natural environment to their advantage, using melted snow for drinking water and building things from ice. Their ice houses (igloos) can be put up in a few hours. The Inuit rely on dogs to pull their sleds great distances. Remains of these dogs, preserved in the snow, show that the Inuit have used these animals for at least 1,000 years.

Where is the coldest place

There are many very cold places on Earth—the Arctic, the Antarctic, Greenland, Canada, Siberia in Russia, for example. The coldest temperatures of all (around –130°F / –90°C) are recorded in the Antarctic. The coldest place where people manage to live is in Siberia.

Some of the coldest places on Earth are found around the North Pole

What is a blizzard

A blizzard occurs when the wind blows at the same time that it is snowing. It makes the snowfall much more dangerous because nothing can be seen in the swirling snow (sometimes called a whiteout). Blizzards also pile the snow up against houses and cars, making it difficult, or impossible, to get out.

When does the sea freeze

At the North and South Poles, part of the sea freezes solid every year and special ships called icebreakers are needed to smash a passage through it. In Europe, very cold weather can make the sea freeze at the edges. Rivers can also gain a thick layer of ice. In fact, years ago, the River Thames in London used to freeze over on a regular basis and a fair used to be held on it. The last of these Frost Fairs took place in February, 1814.

Once an igloo is built, it makes a surprisingly warm home!

EXTREME HEAT

While one part of the world experiences snow or floods for most of the time, other parts may not experience rain for ten years or more. A town in Chile, South America, experienced the longest drought ever—a staggering 400 years!

Where is the hottest place

Africa, Death Valley in California, and Australia are well-known for experiencing extreme heat. In 1917, the temperature in Death Valley averaged 120°F (48°C) on 43 consecutive days in July and August. The town of Dallol in Ethiopia has an incredible average temperature of 93.2°F (34°C). This calculation takes into account the freezing night-time temperatures as well as the boiling daytime ones!

ETHIOPIA

What is a desert

A desert is a place that has very little growing in it, mainly due to very low rainfall. Deserts can be classified in four ways. Those found in Ethiopia are true deserts —hot, dry and sandy. Semi arid deserts in Utah are more humid. Coastal deserts, like the Atacama in Chile, have harsh, rocky areas. Cold deserts, like those of Greenland and Antarctica, can experience snow—but usually less than 2 in. (5 cm) per year.

What is a sandstorm

Apart from the blistering heat, travelers in sandy deserts may also experience terrifying sandstorms, where the arrival of gale force winds can lift the sand into huge walls that swirl upwards and fill the sky, blocking the Sun. Sometimes, the force of the sand blowing around is so strong that it can crackle with electricity. Sandstorms can last for hours, smothering people and their belongings.

Ethiopia in Africa is one of the hottest countries on Earth

Why is a desert cold at night

This seems like a puzzle, but has a simple explanation. There are very few clouds in the sky above a desert, so there is nothing to screen the Sun's heat. Without them, the ground warms up very quickly, but at night it loses its heat because there are no clouds above to trap the warmth. The Sahara experiences temperatures of 130°F (54.5°C) during the day, but is freezing at night.

What is an oasis

An oasis is a place where water can be found in an otherwise dry desert. It happens when the water table (the area below which the ground is saturated) comes to the surface, providing a welcome drink. The water may come to the surface in the form of a spring, and artificial oases have been made in some deserts by forcing groundwater up through wells. An oasis can be the size of a pond (typically surrounded by palm trees) or as large as the desert cities which have been built around these more fertile areas.

FACT FILE

Light rays traveling through the air in a desert pass from cooler, heavier air on the ground to lighter air further up. This causes the light to bend, and causes a "shimmering" effect that looks like water. This is the "mirage" that desert travelers may commonly experience when the air is warm enough.

What is the largest desert

The Sahara in North Africa is the world's biggest desert. It takes up around 8 percent of the world's land area and, contrary to popular belief, it is only covered in 30 percent sand—the rest is gravel and other soils. Also impressive is the Arabian Desert, with 25 percent of its area being unbroken sand. It stretches from Yemen to the Persian Gulf and Oman to Jordan and Iraq.

Animals take advantage of an oasis

What have camels got in their humps

Not water! A camel's hump is made of fat. Camels are able to go for many days without eating or drinking, living off the fat stored in these humps. That is why they make such ideal animals for desert transport, earning them their famous nickname "ships of the desert".

AFRICA

The world's second largest continent is home to jungles and deserts, and some of the world's most amazing animals. The people live in large cities as well as in tribes that live by ancient traditions.

What would you see traveling north to south

Going from north to south, you would start at the beautiful blue Mediterranean Sea. That would give way to the burning sands of the Sahara Desert which go on for hundreds of miles. Around the middle of Africa, the scenery would change to thick rainforest with tall trees and lush vegetation. After that, you would be out on the savannah, the huge open plains where all the famous wild animals live. Finally, you would end up in South Africa, a rich and fertile country with huge farms that grow apples, oranges and grapes for making wine.

South Africa is fertile

Crossing the Sahara

FACT FILE

AFRICA—Essential Fact File

- Area: 11,5831 square miles (30,319,000 square kilometers)

- Number of countries: 53

- Largest country: Sudan (area— 967,500 square miles/ 2,505,800 square kilometers)

- Smallest country: The Gambia (area— 4,362 square miles/ 11,300 square kilometers)

- Longest river: The Nile— 4,157 miles (6,690 kilometers)

- Highest mountain: Mount Kilimanjaro in Tanzania, 19,340 feet (5,895 meters) above sea level

Sailing boats on the River Nile

Algiers

Tunis

Rabat

MOROCCO

TUNISIA

Tripoli

ALGERIA

LIBYA

Cairo

EGYPT

Sudan is the largest country in Africa

WESTERN SAHARA

MAURITANIA

MALI

Nouakchott

NIGER

CHAD

SUDAN

Nile R.

Khartoum

ERITREA

Asmara

Senegal R.

SENEGAL

Niamey

N'Djamena

DJIBOUTI

Djibouti

GAMBIA

Bamako

BURKINA FASO

Ouagadougou

NIGERIA

Chari R.

SOMALIA

GUINEA BISSAU

GUINEA

Conakry

GHANA

BENIN

TOGO

Abuja

CAMEROON

CENTRAL AFRICAN REPUBLIC

Addis Ababa

ETHIOPIA

Freetown

SIERRA LEONE

IVORY COAST

Porto Novo

Benue R.

LIBERIA

Monrovia

Abidjan

Accra

Niger R.

Mogadishu

EQUATORIAL GUINEA

Bangui

CONGO

UGANDA

KENYA

Libreville

GABON

Kampala

RWANDA

Kigali

Nairobi

Gambia is the smallest country in Africa

Brazzaville

Kinshasa

DEM. REP. OF CONGO

Congo R.

Kwilu R.

BURUNDI

Bujumbura

Lake Victoria

Kilimanjaro

TANZANIA

Dar es Salaam

Luanda

ANGOLA

MALAWI

Lilongwe

MOZAMBIQUE

ZAMBIA

Lusaka

Harare

Victoria Falls

ZIMBABWE

MADAGASCAR

Antananarivo

NAMIBIA

Windhoek

BOTSWANA

Kalahari Desert

Africa is the world's second largest continent and is divided into 53 different countries

Gaborone

Pretoria

Maputo

Mbabane

SWAZILAND

Orange R.

Bloemfontein

LESOTHO

Maseru

SOUTH AFRICA

INDIAN

OCEAN

Cape Town

Which animals live in Africa

On the savannah, you would see the following (among others)—

- Zebras • Giraffes • Elephants • Lions
- Cheetahs • Hyenas • Hippopotamuses
- Rhinoceroses

Sadly, many of the wonderful creatures have been hunted to the point that they now face extinction.

Zebra

Lion

Rhino

Take a safari to view some of Africa's spectacular wildlife

Which crops grow in Africa

These crops are grown in plantations and much of them are sold and exported (taken out) of the country so that other countries can buy them.

- Cocoa • Tea • Coffee • Fruit • Cotton

Africa also exports massive quantities of palm oil which is used to make soap and margarine spread.

The African climate is perfect for growing fruit

ASIA

Asia makes up nearly one-third of the world's total land mass. Both the world's highest and lowest points can be found here. Touched by four oceans and covering a huge area, the population is as diverse as the landscape.

Rice grows in water-filled terraces called paddyfields

What food is grown in Asia

Rice is the staple diet of the people of Asia. It grows in layered, water-filled terraces called paddy fields. Wheat for making bread is also important.

The following crops are grown, then sold abroad— tea, cotton, rubber, jute, fruit and tobacco.

FACT FILE

ASIA—Essential Fact File

- Area: 16,9885 square miles (44,418,500 square kilometers)

- Number of countries: 47

- Largest country: China

- Country with the largest number of people: China (followed by India)

- Important rivers: The Tigris, Euphrates, Indus, Ganges and Yangtze

- Highest mountain: Everest

- Fascinating feature: Lake Baikal in Russia. It is the deepest lake in the world and contains a fifth of all the fresh water on the planet!

- Total population: 3,800 million

ARCTIC
OCEAN

Moscow ★

RUSSIA

Siberia

Ob   *Yenisey*

Lake Baikal

Ulaanbaatar ★

★ Tokyo

JAPAN

TURKEY

GEORGIA
ARMENIA
AZERBAIJAN
AZERBAIJAN

CYPRUS
LEBANON
ISRAEL
JORDAN
SYRIA

KAZAKHSTAN

UZBEKISTAN

MONGOLIA

Beijing ★

NORTH
KOREA

★ Pyongyang

SOUTH
KOREA

PACIF

OCEA

Caspian
Sea

L. Balkhash

TURKMENISTAN

Tashkent ★
Ashgabat ★

Bishkek ★

KYRGYZSTAN

Seoul
★

IRAQ Baghdad ★

Dead Sea

★ Tehran

Dushanbe ★

TAJIKISTAN

Euphrates

KUWAIT

AFGHANISTAN

IRAN

Kabul ★

CHINA

Mekong

Salween

Yangtze

Riyadh ★

BAHRAIN

QATAR

SAUDI ARABIA

U. A. E.

★ Muscat

PAKISTAN

Indus

Islamabad ★

New
Delhi ★

NEPAL Kathmandu ★

★ BHUTAN

Mount Everest ▲

Ganges BANGLADESH

VIETNAM

Hanoi ★

LAOS

Vientiane ★

Sanaa ★

YEMEN

OMAN

INDIA

Dhaka ★

Rangoon
★

THAILAND

Bangkok ★

Phnom Penh ★

*Asia makes up nearly
a third of the world's
total land mass*

SRI LANKA

Colombo ★

INDIAN

OCEAN

Sumatra

Kuala Lumpur ★

MALAYSIA

SINGAPORE

Jakarta

Where did man evolve

Modern man (proper name Homo sapiens) evolved in Africa, but the first organized towns, cities and empires (called civilizations) developed in Asia. Amongst the earliest civilizations were those around the Tigris and Euphrates rivers in what is now Iraq, in ancient China and along the Indus Valley of modern Pakistan.

Which animals live in Asia

There are a large number of different animals living in Asia. The Asiatic (also called Indian) lion roams India, feeding on animals such as wild pig and sambar (an Asian deer). India is also home to 60 percent of the world's tigers. The Asian elephant can be found across India and Sri Lanka and as far southeast as Sumatra. Moose roam the Arctic coast, and the famous giant panda lives in the mountains of central China.

A giant panda   **A tiger**

Why is the Dead Sea so called

Because nothing can live in it! This huge lake contains seven times as much salt as normal water. The salt in the Dead Sea makes it much denser than freshwater or normal salt water, so it can support and make you float! The Dead Sea is the lowest area on Earth's surface, at nearly 1,312 feet (400 meters) below sea level.

Floating away in the Dead Sea...

ANTARCTICA

FACT FILE

Antarctica—Essential Fact File

- Area: 5,400,000 square miles (13,824,000 square kilometers)
- Number of countries: None!
- Thickness of the ice: 8,202–15,748 feet (2,500–4,800 meters)
- Abundance of ice: Ninety percent of the world's ice is found in the Antarctic

- Coldest temperature: −128.6°F (−89.2°C) recorded in 1983
- Population: Nil
- Animal life: Penguins, seals and whales
- Continent is made from two massive ice plates, the east and west Antarctic Ice Sheets.
- The "Poles" are simply names for the top and bottom of our planet

The fifth largest continent, Antarctica, has no countries or inhabitants. Scientists stay temporarily to discover more about this land of snow and ice. The South Pole is colder than the North Pole (in the Arctic) because it is surrounded by ice, whereas the North is enclosed by water which has an insulating effect. The warmest it ever gets is 32°F (0°C)!

GRAH
LAN

Deceptior
Island

Bellings
Se

Who was Captain Scott ?

In 1912, two teams of explorers, one from Norway and one from Britain, raced each other to the South Pole. The Norwegian team, led by Roald Amundsen,

Captain Scott

got there first. The British team, led by Robert Falcon Scott, arrived at the Pole only to find the Norwegian flag already flying there. Overcome by exhaustion and hunger, Scott's team didn't survive the journey back—they all died in the frozen wilderness.

QUEEN MAUD LAND

ENDERBY
LAND

Weddell Sea

Davis Sea

PALMER
LAND

RONNE
ICE SHELF

Antarctica

PRINCESS
ELIZABETH LAND

*Vinson Massif
(16,050 ft)*

SOUTH POLE .

ELLSWORTH
LAND

Amundsen-
Scott Station ★

★ Vostok

*Mount Kirkpatrick
(14,856 ft)*

MARIE BYRD
LAND

ROSS ICE
SHELF

WILKES LAND

★ McMurdo Station

THE DRY
VALLEYS

Ross Sea

SOUTH MAGNETIC POLE

*Antarctica has no
countries or inhabitants*

What kind of animals live in the Antarctic

All the big ones! The elephant seal, which is over 20 feet (6 meters) long, lives here, along with the gray seal and the leopard seal. The emperor penguin (3.8 feet tall/1.1 meters) is the largest of the penguin species found in the Antarctic. Among the various whales in the sea is the gigantic blue whale, the largest living mammal on Earth.

The leopard seal is so called because of its distinctive markings. Its only natural predator is the killer whale

Is there a hole above Antarctica

Man's excessive use of gases and chemicals is thought to have weakened the ozone layer (which protects us from the Sun's heat). Scientists have observed a large "hole" in the atmosphere above Antarctica, in the months of September and October. However, it is simply the very low temperatures in the atmosphere over the area that cause this. When summer arrives (December to January) the air above Antarctica is mixed with the world's atmosphere and the hole "repairs" itself. Worryingly though, the "hole", first observed in the 1970s, has become bigger each year.

Emperor penguins are social birds who huddle, taking turns to move to the center for warmth

Blue whales breathe through blowholes, which can be heard for miles around the Antarctic

AUSTRALASIA

Every part of Australasia, the smallest continent (made up of Australia, New Zealand and various Pacific islands), is surrounded by ocean. This affects the climate here. Australia is generally mild all year round, whereas Papua New Guinea is hot and tropical and most of New Zealand has a warm and wet climate.

What does Australasia produce ❓

Much of Australia contains vast swathes of barren desert. The population tends to live in cities around the coast. The rest of the country consists of grassy plains and highlands which are ideal for keeping cattle and sheep. Australia has millions of sheep—the country produces one third of all the wool used in the whole world. New Zealand is also a great sheep-rearing country, but their better-quality grazing land means that the animals are raised for meat which is frozen and sold abroad.

FACT FILE

AUSTRALASIA—Essential Fact File

- Countries: Australia, New Zealand, Fiji, Papua New Guinea and many other Pacific islands and island chains. (Total number recognized as proper countries: 11)

- Area (Australia only): 2,70272 square miles (7,687,000 square kilometers)

- States (Australia only): New South Wales, Victoria, Queensland, South Australia, Tasmania, Northern Territory and Western Australia

- Highest mountain: Puncak Jaya, New Guinea—16,503 feet (5,030 meters)

- Features: Uluru (also known as Ayers Rock), Great Barrier Reef

Uluru

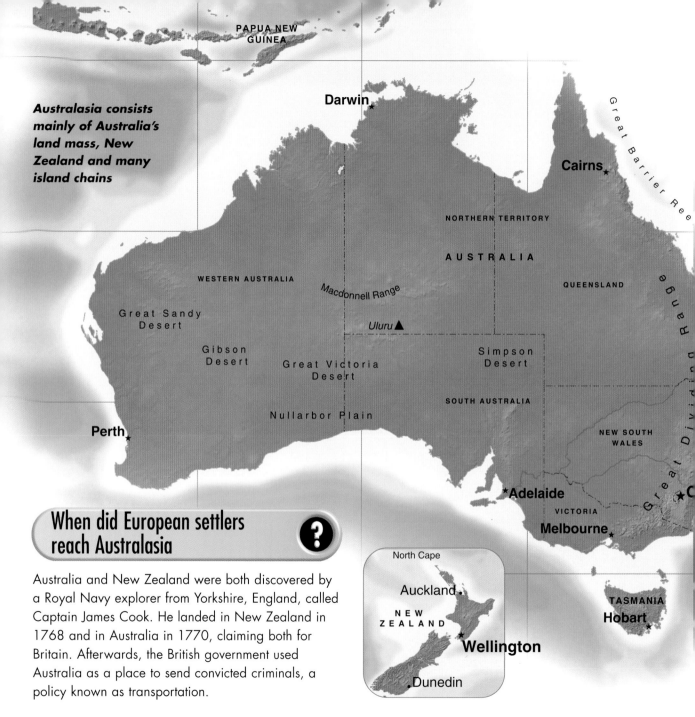

Australasia consists mainly of Australia's land mass, New Zealand and many island chains

PAPUA NEW GUINEA

Darwin ★

Cairns ★

Great Barrier Ree

NORTHERN TERRITORY

AUSTRALIA

WESTERN AUSTRALIA

Macdonnell Range

Great Sandy Desert

Uluru ▲

Gibson Desert

Great Victoria Desert

Simpson Desert

QUEENSLAND

Great Dividing Range

SOUTH AUSTRALIA

Nullarbor Plain

Perth ★

NEW SOUTH WALES

★Adelaide

VICTORIA

Melbourne ★

C

When did European settlers reach Australasia ❓

Australia and New Zealand were both discovered by a Royal Navy explorer from Yorkshire, England, called Captain James Cook. He landed in New Zealand in 1768 and in Australia in 1770, claiming both for Britain. Afterwards, the British government used Australia as a place to send convicted criminals, a policy known as transportation.

North Cape

Auckland ●

NEW ZEALAND

Wellington ★

● Dunedin

TASMANIA

Hobart ★

Who are the Aborigines and the Maoris ❓

Aborigines are the native people of Australia. Maoris are the native people of New Zealand. Both lived in their respective countries for thousands of years before the arrival of white European settlers. It is believed that Aborigines made their way from Asia at least 30,000 years ago. Today, they make up approximately 2.6 percent of the Australian population.

Brisbane

dney

ra

What are the famous sights ❓

The Great Barrier Reef is the largest coral reef in the world, extending over 1,243 miles (2,000 kilometers) off the northern shore of Queensland, Australia. Coral is a living stone made up of billions of tiny animals called coral polyps. This beautiful underwater landscape is in danger of dying off due to pollution in the water.

Uluru (also known as Ayers Rock) is the biggest monolith (single block of stone) in the world. Found in the desert in the center of Australia it rises 1,142 feet (348 meters) above the ground.

EUROPE

The sixth largest continent, Europe is formed from many countries, each with its own culture. This makes it a diverse place to visit.

What is the climate like in Europe

In the north, countries like Norway and Finland receive a lot of snow and have frozen territory inside the Arctic Circle. To the south, countries like Spain, Italy and Greece bask in hot sunshine for many months, and are vacation favorites. Eastern countries such as Hungary have warm summers but much colder winters.

Mediterranean heat.

Frozen territory!

Which city has the most people

The most highly populated cities in Europe include Moscow in Russia, Istanbul in Turkey and London in England.

Which is the biggest country

Russia is the biggest country in Europe. The smallest is The Vatican, the Pope's palace in Rome. Even though it is only 0.17 square miles (0.44 square kilometers), it is classified as a separate country!

Shetland
Islands

Orkney
Islands

Hebrides

FINLAND

NORWAY

Helsinki ★

Oslo ★
Stockholm ★   Baltic   ★ Tallinn
SWEDEN   Sea   ESTONIA

Moscow ★

Riga ★   LATVIA

IRELAND   DENMARK   LITHUANIA
Dublin ★   North Sea   ★ Copenhagen   Kaunas ★   Volga
U. K.   RUSS.
                      FED.   Minsk ★   RUSSIA
London ★   Amsterdam★   BELARUS
       NETH.   Berlin ★   POLAND
Brussels ★   GERMANY   ★ Warsaw   Kiev ★
BELGIUM
Paris ★   LUX.   ★ Prague   UKRAINE
       Rhine   CZECH REPUBLIC
Bay   FRANCE   Vienna ★ SLOVAKIA MOLDOVA
of   Bern ★ AUSTRIA ★Bratislava Chisinau ★
Biscay   SWITZERLAND ★Budapest   Mount Elbrus ▲
              Ljubljana★ HUNGARY
              SLOVENIA ★Zagreb   ROMANIA   Black Sea
Monaco ★   Adriatic CROATIA   ★ Bucharest
ANDORRA   Sea BOSNIA ★Belgrade
                   Danube SERBIA BULGARIA
PORTUGAL   ITALY ★Sarajevo
Lisbon ★ ★ Madrid   MONTENEGRO ★ KOSOVO★ Sofia
SPAIN   Corsica   Podgorica★Pristina
Majorca   Tirane★ ★ Skopje
Sardinia   Rome ★   ALBANIA MACEDONIA

Sicily   GREECE
                    ★ Athens
Mediterranean   Crete
     Sea   CYPRUS

What does Mediterranean mean ?

The name Mediterranean means "in the middle of the land". In ancient times, it was literally the center of the known world. Western culture began here with the Greeks and Romans and we still follow many of the laws and customs that they laid down. In particular, we use their form of government in which people choose their leaders by voting. This is known as democracy.

Europe is made up of many diverse countries

Many European countries are run democratically

NORTH AMERICA

The third largest continent is formed from the larger countries of Canada, Mexico and the United States, the countries of Central America and the Caribbean islands. The land is diverse, from the harsh conditions of the Arctic Circle to the tropical beaches of Florida. There's even some desert!

FACT FILE

NORTH AMERICA— Essential Fact File

- Area: 9,266,450 square miles (24,240,000 square kilometers)
- Number of countries: 23
- Main mountains: The Rockies
- Main rivers: Mississippi, St Lawrence, Rio Grande and Colorado
- Main lakes: Superior, Michigan, Huron, Erie and Ontario (The Great Lakes)
- Population: 528 million
- Most famous feature: Niagara Falls

Who was Christopher Columbus

This Italian explorer was credited with discovering the Americas. He made four voyages, landing on the American mainland in 1498. He thought he had reached India. That is why the big islands south of Florida are called the West Indies and Native Americans have, until recently, been known as Indians. However, it is now known that the Vikings were the first Europeans to reach America, having sailed there several centuries earlier.

Christopher Columbus

ARCTIC
OCEAN

GREENLAND

Yukon

Nuuk
(Godthab)

Rocky
Mountains

Mackenzie

Great Bear Lake

Great Slave Lake

Lake Athabasca

CANADA

Hudson
Bay

★ Edmonton

Vancouver

Calgary

Seattle

Lake Winnipeg

Missouri

Rocky Mountains

Montreal

Lake Nipigon

Lake Superior

★ Ottawa

Lake Huron

Great Lakes

Lake Ontario

Rochester   Cape Cod

San Francisco

Lake Michigan

Minneapolis

Toronto

Milwaukee

Niagara
Falls

Mississippi

Detroit

Chicago

Cleveland

New York

Philadelphia

Kansas City

Lake Erie

Baltimore

Grand Canyon

UNITED STATES
OF AMERICA

Ohio

★ Washington D. C.

Los Angeles

Great Plains

San Diego

Sierra Madre Occidental

Death
Valley

Memphis

Appalachian Mts.

ATLANTIC

OCEAN

Mississippi

Birmingham

Dallas

Jacksonville

Rio Grande

Houston

New Orleans

Tampa

Miami

MEXICO

BAHAMAS

Gulf of Mexico

Nassau

Havana

CUBA

Port-au-Prince   DOM. REP.

Mexico City

Santo Domingo

HAITI

Belmopan

★ JAMAICA

BELIZE

Kingston

GUATEMALA   HONDURAS

Guatemala ★   ★ Tegucigalpa

San Salvador

NICARAGUA

EL SALVADOR

COSTA
RICA

★ Panama

*North America
covers 9,266,450 square
miles (24,240,000
square kilometers)—
slightly larger than
Brazil and about half
the size of Russia*

What is there to see in North America

Everything is said to be big in America and it certainly has its own share of "biggest and best"—

- Lake Superior is the world's largest freshwater lake
- Greenland is the world's largest island
- The world's tallest trees are found in California
- The Rocky Mountains are the world's second longest mountain range
- The Mississippi River is the fourth longest river in the world

The Mississippi River

The Rockies

What are the Great Lakes

The five lakes near the border of Canada and the United States are really vast inland seas which cover an area of 750 miles (1,200 kilometers). In terms of volume, the largest is Lake Superior, followed by Michigan, Huron, Ontario and Erie.

What are the famous sites

Niagara Falls is a spectacular waterfall that sees almost half a million tons of water plunge over a 164 feet (50 meter) drop every minute! This massive amount of water comes from the Great Lakes just to the north.

The Grand Canyon is the deepest gorge in the world. (A gorge is a deep valley cut by a river.) Created by the Colorado river in Arizona, the Canyon has some breathtaking scenery and, like Niagara Falls, is a famous tourist attraction.

Niagara Falls

The Grand Canyon

SOUTH AMERICA

South America is the fourth largest continent, and its countries display a great variety of climates. There's the wet, tropical Amazon rainforest in Brazil, the humid subtropical temperatures of Argentina and the dry mountain air of Peru.

SOUTH AMERICA— Essential Fact File

- Area: 6,563,74 square miles (17,830,000 square kilometers)

- Number of countries: 13

- Biggest country: Brazil (covers half of the whole continent)

- Main mountains: the Andes

- Main rivers: the Amazon, Orinoco and the joint River Plate–Paraguay–Parana

- Population: 382 million

- Famous feature: the Amazon rainforest

What exactly is a rainforest

In rainforests, lots of trees grow close together, the tops of which are called crowns. Some trees grow to 200 feet (61 meters) and form the upper canopy, which is home to many types of wildlife, including the sloth (below). Shorter trees, which form the other layers of the canopy, help to block out the light, so that relatively little grows on the rainforest floor. Rainforests are different to jungles, which receive a lot of sunlight, and have areas of dense growth on the ground (often found near swamps).

The rainforests of South America are home to many species of wildlife, including the parrot, sloth and tarantula

South America is the fourth largest continent

Barranquilla

Caracas

Valencia

Orinoco

Medellin

Bogota

VENEZUELA

Georgetown

Paramaribo

COLOMBIA

SURINAME

Cayenne

Quito

GUYANA

FRENCH
GUIANA

ECUADOR

Negro

Belem

Manaus

Amazon

Fortaleza

PERU

Madeira

Recife

Pacific

Ocean

Lima

BOLIVIA

BRAZIL

Salvador

Goiania

Brasilia

La Paz

Mato Grosso

Sucre

Plateau

Belo Horizonte

PARAGUAY

Rio de
Janeiro

Sao Paulo

Asuncion

Curitiba

ARGENTINA

Porto
Alegre

Rosario

URUGUAY

Santiago

Buenos Aires

Montevideo

CHILE

Atlantic

Ocean

FALKLAND
ISLANDS

Stanley

Tierra Del Fuego

What is special about the Andes

It is the longest mountain range in the world. The mountains start up in the north in Colombia and run right down the Pacific coast to Patagonia, a distance of about 4,970 miles (8,000 kilometers). Their highest point is Mount Aconcagua in Argentina which is 22,864 feet (6,969 meters) above sea level.

What is the Amazon basin

The Amazon river starts in the Andes mountains and flows right through South America for a distance of 4,000 miles (6,437 kilometers). Over the centuries, this mighty river has carved out a wide, flat area either side which is known as its basin. Much of the Amazon basin is covered by tropical rainforest.

The Amazon starts in the Andes

What does Brazil produce

The flat-to-rolling land and mainly tropical climate leads to the successful growth of coffee, cocoa, sugar and soya beans, and Brazil exports a lot of these products. The majority of coffee beans produced for export come from the arabica bush, which bears fruit containing two seeds.

FACT FILE

The most spoken languages in South America are Spanish and Portuguese. Portuguese is the official language of Brazil, whilst Spanish is for most of the other countries.

Deforestation

Why are rare animals in danger

In many parts of South America, the cutting and burning of trees takes place in order to clear land for livestock to graze and crops to be planted. This process is known as deforestation. Once these areas of the rainforest have been cleared, the animals and plants lose their habitat and may become extinct. There is pressure on these countries to gain income through other methods, and to leave the natural world intact.

SUN AND MOON

The Moon orbits Earth, and Earth orbits the Sun. When these paths cross, we can witness wonderful sights. Even our little Moon has some control over us...

How does the Moon cause tides

As the Moon orbits Earth, its gravitational field pulls Earth's water towards it. Earth is turning at the same time, interrupting the pull. This causes two high and two low tides every day. High tide is when the ocean flows as far inland as possible, low tide is when it flows as far as it can from land.

What are solar and lunar eclipses

A solar eclipse occurs when the Moon passes in front of the Sun, casting its shadow on part of Earth. A lunar eclipse is the opposite—Earth passes in front of the Sun and casts its shadow on part of the Moon. A rare total solar eclipse happens when Earth and the Moon line up, blocking the Sun temporarily. Although they occur somewhere on Earth, on average, every 18 months, scientists estimate that they recur in the same place once every 370 years. They only last a few minutes at a time. Unlike a total solar eclipse, a lunar eclipse can be viewed anywhere that is on the "night" side of the world. This type of eclipse lasts a few hours and are more common than total solar eclipses.

Why does the Moon appear to be the same size as the Sun

The Moon is 237,364 miles (382,000 kilometers) from Earth, and can be reached by space rockets. The Sun, however, is 92,584,300 miles (149,598,020 kilometers) away. So, although the Moon is 400 times smaller than the Sun, they seem the same size in the sky.

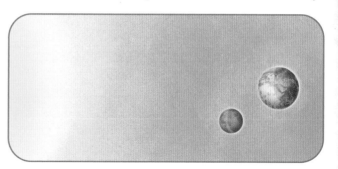

The Moon is much closer to Earth than the Sun

FACT FILE

An eclipse viewed from Earth lasts for only a few minutes. From the air, however, its time can be greatly extended by following the eclipse round the world in a fast-moving aircraft like Concorde.

What is the Sun's corona

During a total solar eclipse, the Moon passes exactly in front of the Sun and, for a few minutes, you can see only the Sun's halo of glowing gases, called the corona (meaning "crown"). Scientists are unsure why these rays at the edge of the Sun, shooting off into the atmosphere, are actually hotter than the Sun's surface (the photosphere).

A total solar eclipse is rare.
You are likely to only see one in your lifetime.

How big is the Moon's shadow

During a solar eclipse, the dark shadow that the Moon casts on Earth's surface is a circle about 168 miles (270 kilometers) across. It is called the umbra. A much lighter shadow (about 1,864 miles / 3,000 kilometers across) surrounds the umbra.

The Moon casts a shadow called the umbra

WARNING

You should not look at an eclipse with a telescope, the naked eye, or even through sunglasses as the Sun's light could cause damage to your eyes. However, it is possible to view an eclipse safely through a pinhole camera.

NATURAL WONDERS

Our planet has many beautiful places which have breathtaking natural features and awe-inspiring scenery. Here's a look at the top six which maybe you'll be lucky enough to visit one day...

The Victoria Falls

On the border of Zimbabwe and Zambia, the falls are known locally as the "Mosi-oa-Tunya" ("smoke that thunders"). The seven waterfalls occur when the Zambezi river plunges 354 feet (108 meters) down several series of basalt gorges.

Mauna Loa

This is the world's largest active volcano. It is so large that it takes up half the area of Hawaii. The top point is a massive 13,681 feet (4,170 meters) high. The large crater at the top, named Mokuaweoweo Caldera, can be clearly seen from space! Scientists believe it started to form nearly one million years ago.

Yellowstone National Park

This huge protected area in Wyoming spans an area of 3,468 square miles (8,980 km²), and mainly consists of lakes, mountain ranges, rivers and canyons. It is also home to the biggest natural geysers in the world. See the scalding hot water shooting into the sky at regular intervals.

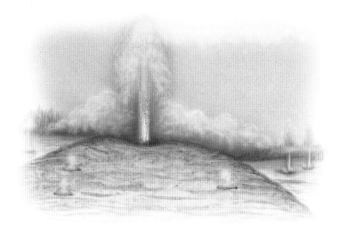

Great Barrier Reef

The world's largest coral reef, this is an underwater world of astonishing color and beauty. It is located off the coast of northeast Australia and is built by billions of tiny organisms, as well as home to a wide diversity of life—from fish to turtles.

Mount Everest

Arguably the world's greatest natural wonder, it is the tallest of the many snow-capped Himalayan peaks that seem to reach up and touch the sky. Its summit is 29,029 feet (8,848 meters)!

The Grand Canyon

Located in Arizona, the scenery here is so awesome that you feel small just looking at it! The Grand Canyon is 277 miles (446 km) long, 4–18 miles (6.4–29 km) wide and over a mile (6,000 feet) deep. The gorge was carved out by the Colorado River around 17 million years ago. The river has continued to erode the magnificent natural wonder to form the gorge as it is today.

GLOSSARY

Aborigine
A native of Australia who was living there when European settlers arrived.

Aftershocks
Tremors following an earthquake.

Arid
Description of a place that has little or no rain.

Atmosphere
The gassy area surrounding Earth, split into five layers.

Aurora borealis
The "northern lights"— spectacular light displays mainly seen in the night skies of the most northern hemisphere.

Avalanche
A large fall of snow and ice down a mountain.

Basin
Where a river and its tributaries join together and are "captured".

Beaufort Scale
An international scale used to measure wind speeds.

Billion
A billion is a thousand million. Written as a number it is 1,000,000,000.

Brackish
Slightly salty water— usually found where a river meets the sea.

Climate
The type of weather that is typical (long term) of an area.

Condensation
The process in which gas becomes compressed into either a liquid or solid state.

Crater
The cone-shaped mountain built up by a volcano, often with an open top. If the volcano is still active, lava will bubble in the crater.

Dead Sea
The lowest area of water on Earth's surface, so full of salt that it cannot support life.

Delta
The flat area at the end of a river, which has divided into a number of smaller distributaries.

Drought
A long period of low rainfall.

Eclipse
The total or partial obscuring of one celestial body by another.

Electromagnetic waves
The energy which is produced by an electromagnetic field.

Empire
A group of people and land under the rule of a single person or state.

Epicenter
The point immediately above the origin of an earthquake.

Estuary
Where a river reaches the end of its journey— flowing into a sea or lake at a slow speed.

Evaporation
The process by which something more dense changes into something less dense (like a liquid to a gas).

Export
Food, raw materials and manufactured goods that are sold to other countries to make money.

Extinct and Extinction
When a species of animal is about to die out and disappear for ever, it is said to be facing extinction. When this terrible event finally happens, the animal has become extinct.

Faculae
Bright clouds of helium above areas where sunspots form.

Galaxy
A group of stars and planets forming a part of the universe.

Geyser
A spring that discharges steam and hot water.

Global warming
Because of pollution, Earth's atmosphere is getting warmer. This may have serious consequences in the very near future.

Gorge
A deep valley formed by a river.

Gravity
This is the natural force that presses down on the surface of Earth, keeping everything in place.

GLOSSARY

Ice shelf
Found at the Poles, a thick block of ice attached to the land which sticks out and floats into the sea.

Inuit
A native of the Arctic.

Irrigation
The use of water from rivers and lakes to make crops grow.

Jute
Yellow-flowered plants, grown for their strong fibers which can be made into rope and other such products.

Lava
The hot liquid magma spewing from the top or sides of a volcano.

Magma
Hot molten rock within Earth's crust which becomes solid rock if it reaches Earth's surface.

Magnetic field
A field of force surrounding a permanent magnet.

Maori
A Polynesian native living in New Zealand and the Cook Islands.

Molecules
Everything in the world is made of atoms. When these atoms bond together in different ways, the resulting compounds are called molecules.

Monolith
A large block of stone.

Ozone layer
A layer of molecules that forms in the stratosphere. Good at absorbing ultraviolet radiation, it protects life on Earth.

Paddyfields
Layered, water-filled terraces, used for growing rice.

Peninsula
A piece of land that sticks out, joined at one end to another area of land.

Population
The number of inhabitants (usually people) living in a particular place.

Precipitation
Any weather such as rain, snow, sleet or dew, caused by the condensation of water in the atmosphere.

Rainforest
A thick forest found in areas that have heavy rainfall.

Reef
A ridge of rock, sand, coral etc, the top of which lies just under the sea's surface.

Reservoir
A lake which collects and stores water for people to use.

Richter scale
An international scale used to measure the strength of earthquakes.

Sandstorm
A swirling mass of sand, whipped up by the wind.

Seismic
Relating to, or caused by, earthquakes or Earth tremors.

Solar flares
Bright loops of hot gas emerging from areas of the Sun where sunspots are present.

Solar system
This is the name of the group of eight planets, including Earth, that go around the Sun.

Staple diet
A food of prime importance, in terms of consumption and trade.

Static electricity
Electrical energy that builds up in a certain place rather than being "on the move" like other electricity.

Summit
The highest point of a mountain.

Sunspot
A dark area on the Sun's surface.

Supercontinent
A huge piece of land thought to have split into smaller pieces which now form the seven continents.

Tributary
A stream, river or glacier that feeds on another of these.

Umbra
A shadow cast by the Moon on the surface of Earth.

Water cycle
Water circulation, via evaporation, precipitation and condensation.

INDEX